MW01291407

Secret of the Rosary

Publications

To Jesus Through Mary

To the Sorrowful and Immaculate Heart of Mary

This book is presented to the public in the hope that it will inspire the faithful to a deeper devotion and urge them to make known to others the message contained therein. May this book bring souls to the Sorrowful and Immaculate Mother whose pure heart was crushed with sorrow, when she contemplated the sufferings of her Son and the misery of souls remaining untouched by the graces won by Christ on the Cross. Its pages will make Our Lady better known and loved; they will bring into prominence the ardent desire of Our Lord to save the world through the most Sorrowful and Immaculate Heart of His beloved Mother, and that by the fulfillment of the conditions so mercifully offered by the Sacred Heart of Jesus, the salvation and peace of the world may fully be realized.

Berthe Petit, 39 years of age

Words of Divine Love

to Berthe Petit

On the Devotion to the
Sorrowful and Immaculate Heart of Mary

*Compiled from the book, "The Sorrowful and
Immaculate Heart of Mary"*

By Editor, Secret of the Rosary

PUBLISHED, 2005
Secret of the Rosary
U. S. A

About the Front Cover: Photograph of Berthe Petit (at the age of 39) digitally remastered and republished with permission from the Conventual Franciscan Friars of Marytown, Libertyville, Illinois.

Photograph and illustrations digitally remastered and republished with permission from the Conventual Franciscan Friars of Marytown, Libertyville, Illinois.

Quotations compiled from the book, "The Sorrowful and Immaculate Heart of Mary" with permission from the Conventual Franciscan Friars of Marytown, Libertyville, Illinois.

Published 2005
Secret of the Rosary
United States of America

Send all inquiries to:
customerservice@sorrowful-and-immaculate.com
vanschwer@earthlink.com
leevanschwer@hotmail.com

or to:

Editor
Secret of the Rosary
4001 N Oak Lane
Sulphur, La. 70665
U. S. A.

337-558-6523

ISBN: located on back cover

DECLARATION

In obedience to the Decrees of Urban VIII and other Sovereign Pontiffs, the writer declares that for the miraculous events, visions, revelations and apparitions narrated in this book that no other authority or belief is claimed than that which is usually given to narratives resting on merely human evidence. There is no intention to pronounce on their authenticity or supernatural character. If the appellation Saint or Blessed is herein given to any person not canonized or beatified by the Church, it is done so only in accordance with the usage and opinion of men. What is printed herein is mainly historical: the actual facts that occurred and the testimony of the witnesses who observed these facts. The opinions given by the writer are not meant in anyway to presuppose the final judgment of the supreme ecclesiastical hierarchy.

Nevertheless, the documented life of Berthe Petit, along with the numerous favorable testimonies on her character from ecclesiastical authorities, gives credit to the messages that she claims to have received from God. Taken as a whole, these messages are consistent with the pontifical pronouncements and the authentic teaching of the Magisterium of the Church.

PREFACE

The messages listed in this book are taken from, "The Sorrowful and Immaculate Heart of Mary" (published in 2004 by Secret of the Rosary Publications). The above book is recommended reading for providing the background and context for the messages in this publication.

In this present book, the messages have been extracted, compiled and categorized in order to present a cohesive continuity and to provide an enhanced clarity to the main overall messages. A chronological list of messages to Berthe Petit are listed in Chapter 6 as a reference guide.

Care has been taken not to add any commentaries or insertions that might change the content of the messages.

Editor, Secret of the Rosary

L'APPROBATION DU VOCABLE

«Cœur douloureux et immaculé de Marie»

Suprema Sacra Congregatio
    Sancti Officii
Prot. N 440/IO

Ex Aedibus S. Offici die
21 augusti 1958

Excellence Révérendissime,

Au mois de juillet dernier, Votre Excellence Révérendissime soumettait à la considération du Saint-Office une question concernant la dévotion au Coeur Douloureux et Immaculé de Marie. Et plus précisément vous demandiez si le Saint-Office ne voyait pas d'inconvénients dans la position actuelle des adjectifs, ou bien s'il était nécessaire de les intervertir.

Cette suprême S.Congrégation, après avoir examiné la demande, a retenu que la position actuelle des mots, c'est-à-dire Coeur Douloureux et Immaculé de Marie peut être gardée intacte, parce qu'elle ne présente aucun inconvénient.

Veuillez agréer, Excellence, l'expression de mes hommages très respectueux et dévoués.

(signé : J.Card. Pizzardo

Secr.

Son Excellence Révérendissime
Monseigneur Auguste Joseph Gaudel
Evêque de Fréjus et Toulon
à TOULON (Var)

CONTENTS

I. The Mission of Berthe Petit: Consecration of the World to the Sorrowful and Immaculate Heart of Mary

Compiled from the Messages to Berthe Petit

On February, 1910 while on pilgrimage to St. Anne's in Alsace, it was revealed to Berthe Petit that her mission would be the **Consecration of the World to the Sorrowful and Immaculate Heart of Mary.**

Our Lord said words: "The world must be consecrated to the Sorrowful and Immaculate Heart of My Mother as it is to Mine. Fear nothing, no matter what obstacle or suffering you may encounter; your only object must be the accomplishment of My Will."

And in a later message. . .

"It is hearts that must be changed. This will be accomplished only by the Devotion proclaimed, explained, preached and recommended everywhere. Recourse to My Mother under the title I wish for her universally, *is the last help I shall give before the end of time.*"

II. Sermon on the Sorrowful and Immaculate Heart of Mary by the Sacred Heart of Jesus Christ

Compiled from the Messages (1909 – 1942)

"The Heart of My Mother has the right to be called *Sorrowful* and I wish this title placed *before* that of *Immaculate* because She has won it Herself. The Church has defined in the case of My Mother what I Myself had ordained — Her Immaculate Conception. This right which My Mother has to a title of justice, is now, according to My express wish, to be known and universally accepted. She has earned it by Her identification with My sorrows, by Her sufferings: by Her sacrifices and Her immolation on Calvary endured in perfect correspondence with My grace for the salvation of mankind."

"The title of Immaculate belongs to the whole being of My Mother and not specially to Her Heart. This title flows from my gratuitous gift to the Virgin who was to give me birth. My Mother has acquired for her Heart the title of Sorrowful by sharing generously in all the sufferings of My Heart and My Body from the crib to the cross. There is not one of these Sorrows which did not pierce the Heart of My Mother. Living image of My crucified Body, her virginal flesh bore the invisible marks of My wounds as her Heart felt the Sorrows of My own. Nothing could ever tarnish the incorruptibility of her Immaculate Heart."

"The title of 'Sorrowful' belongs therefore to the Heart of My Mother, and more than any other, this title is dear to Her because it springs from the union of her Heart with Mine in the redemption of humanity. This title has been acquired by her through her full participation in My Calvary, and it precedes the gratuitous title 'Immaculate' which My love bestowed upon her by a singular privilege. By her acceptance of Calvary My Mother has participated in all My sufferings. Devotion to her Heart united to Mine will bring peace, that true peace, so often implored and yet so little merited."

"It is through the Sorrowful and Immaculate Heart of My Mother that I will triumph, because having co-operated in the redemption of souls, this Heart has the right to share a similar co-operation in the manifestations of My justice and of My love. My Mother is noble in everything, but She is especially so in Her wounded Heart, transfixed by the wound of Mine."

"The world must be consecrated to the Sorrowful and Immaculate Heart of My Mother as it is to Mine. Fear nothing, no matter what obstacle or suffering you may encounter; your only object must be the accomplishment of My Will."

"This wish of Mine follows from what I accomplished on Calvary. When I gave John to My Mother as her son, did I not confide the whole world to Her Sorrowful and Immaculate Heart?"

"By confident consecration to My Mother, the Devotion to My Heart will be strengthened and, as it were, completed. This Devotion, this Consecration will be, according to My promise, a renovation for My Church, a renewed strength for Christianity which is too often wavering, a source of signal graces for souls, who thereby will be more deeply penetrated with love and confidence."

"This Devotion to the Sorrowful and Immaculate Heart of My Mother will restore faith and hope to broken hearts and to ruined families: it will help to repair the destruction: it will sweeten sorrow. It will be a new strength for My Church, bringing souls, not only to confidence in My Heart, but also to abandonment to the Sorrowful Heart of My Mother."

"The safety of your country, internal peace and confidence in My Church will revive through the spread of the Devotion and the Consecration which I wish in order that the Sorrowful and Immaculate Heart of My Mother, united in all to My Heart, may be loved and glorified. Deliverance will thus be the work of our two Hearts, the triumph of our love for the people upon whom this Consecration will bestow confidence according to My promises."

"Desiring for Her Heart a radiant, dazzling, brilliant triumph, I have awaited this time of universal distress which finds an echo in the Sorrowful Heart of My Mother, a Heart universal as My own. To adopt this Devotion and to spread it, is to accomplish My Will and to respond to the wishes of My Heart. Because, by prayer and by the consecration made to this Heart, graces of light will be obtained. They will gradually bring souls to the full knowledge of our united Hearts, which have been wounded by the same wound, the inexhaustible source of all good for humanity, and the glory of which is now, and ever will be, the happiness of the elect for Eternity."

"The clear light to be granted, through recourse to My Mother, will bring about, above all, the conversion of a multitude of straying and sinful souls: the pity of the Sorrowful and Immaculate Heart of My Mother will implore Mercy for them from My Heart."

"Joseph, who supported My Mother and protected My divine Infancy, is your support in a cause which is so dear to him, because he knew many of the sorrows which transfixed My Mother's Heart, and he foresaw, before his death, all that Her Heart would still have to endure."

"The time is now ripe and I wish mankind to turn to the Sorrowful and Immaculate Heart of My Mother. Let this prayer be uttered by every soul: 'Sorrowful and Immaculate Heart of Mary, pray for us.' Let this prayer dictated by My Love as a supreme succor be approved and indulgenced, no longer partially and for a small portion of My flock, but for the whole universe, so that it may spread as a refreshing and purifying balm of reparation that will appease My anger."

"In Her co-redemption lies the nobility of My Mother and for this reason I ask that the Invocation [Sorrowful and Immaculate Heart of Mary, pray for us] which I have demanded be approved and spread through the whole Church. It has already obtained many graces; it will obtain yet more when the Church will be exalted and the world renewed through its Consecration to the Sorrowful and Immaculate Heart of My Mother."

"You must contemplate the Heart of My Mother, as you contemplate My own; live in that Heart as you wish to live in Mine; give yourself to that Heart as you give yourself to Mine; spread the love of Her Heart which is wholly united to Mine. Teach souls to love the Heart of My Mother pierced by the very sorrows which pierced Mine."

"It is My desire that this picture [Sketch of the Vision of the Two Hearts], guided by My hand, be spread far and wide, simultaneously with the invocation. Wherever it will be venerated, My Mercy and My Love will be made manifest and the sight of Our Hearts, wounded by the same wound, will encourage tepid and weak souls to come back to their duty."

4

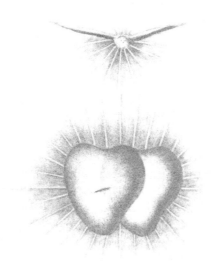

Sketch of the Vision of the Two Hearts

"I have made known to you the wishes of My Heart concerning the Devotion to the Heart of My Mother. Love it and make it loved! This love will be for you and for the whole world a source of grace, and it will bring upon you great blessings. Surrender yourself to My love."

"It is hearts that must be changed. This will be accomplished only by the Devotion proclaimed, explained, preached and recommended everywhere. Recourse to My Mother under the title I wish for her universally, *is the last help I shall give before the end of time.*"

"In the hour of triumph it will be seen that *I alone have inspired,* in my chosen instruments, a Devotion similar to that with which My Heart is honored. IT IS AS A SON THAT I HAVE CONCEIVED THIS DEVOTION IN HONOR OF MY MOTHER. IT IS AS GOD THAT I IMPOSE IT."

III. Messages on the Devotion to the Sorrowful and Immaculate Heart of Mary from the Blessed Virgin Mary

Compiled from the Messages to Berthe Petit

"I have called myself the Immaculate Conception. To you I call myself Mother of the Sorrowful Heart. This title willed by my Son is dear to me above all others. According as it is spread everywhere, there will be granted graces of mercy, spiritual renewal and salvation."

"It is with an unshakable resolve that my Son wills souls to have recourse to my Sorrowful Heart. With my heart overflowing with tenderness, I am awaiting this gesture on the part of souls, that I may reiterate to the Heart of my Son whatever will be confided to my own Heart, and thus obtain graces of salvation for all."

"See here the wound of My Heart, similar to that of my Son, and the torrent of grace ready to gush forth from it . . . . You can now understand the sorrows which my Heart endured, the sufferings of my whole being for the salvation of the world."

IV. PRACTICE OF THE DEVOTION TO THE SORROWFUL AND IMMACULATE HEART OF MARY

Summaries from the Messages (1909 – 1942)

1) "I wish this title [Sorrowful] placed *before* that of *Immaculate* because She has won it Herself. . . This right which My Mother has to a title of justice, is now, according to My express wish, to be known and universally accepted."

2) "The time is now ripe and I wish mankind to turn to the Sorrowful and Immaculate Heart of My Mother. . . The world must be consecrated to the Sorrowful and Immaculate Heart of My Mother as it is to Mine."

3) "The Sorrowful and Immaculate Heart of My Mother, united in all to My Heart, [should be] . . . loved and glorified . . Teach souls to love the Heart of My Mother pierced by the very sorrows which pierced Mine. . . Love [this Heart] it and make it loved!"

4) "Let this prayer be uttered by every soul: '*Sorrowful and Immaculate Heart of Mary, pray for us.*' Let this prayer dictated by My Love as a supreme succor be approved and indulgenced, no longer partially and for a small portion of My flock, but for the whole universe, so that it may spread as a refreshing and purifying balm of reparation that will appease My anger. . . In Her co-redemption lies the nobility of My Mother and for this reason I ask that the Invocation [*Sorrowful and Immaculate Heart of Mary, pray for us*] which I have demanded be approved and spread through the whole Church."

5) "You must contemplate the Heart of My Mother, as you contemplate My own; live in that Heart as you wish to live in Mine; give yourself to that Heart as you give yourself to Mine; spread the love of Her Heart which is wholly united to Mine."

7

6) "It is hearts that must be changed. This will be accomplished only by the Devotion proclaimed, explained, preached and recommended everywhere. . . To adopt this Devotion and to spread it, is to accomplish My Will and to respond to the wishes of My Heart. . . It is as a Son that I have conceived this Devotion in honor of my Mother. It is as God that I impose it."

7) "It is My desire that this picture [Sketch of the Vision of the Two Hearts], guided by My hand, be spread far and wide, simultaneously with the invocation. Wherever it will be venerated, My Mercy and My Love will be made manifest and the sight of Our Hearts, wounded by the same wound, will encourage tepid and weak souls to come back to their duty."

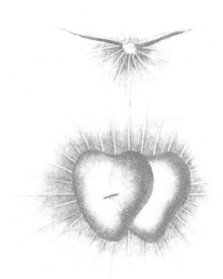

Sketch of the Vision of the Two Hearts

8) "However, in the beginning of 1912, Our Lord made His servant understand. . . that the time had come to make it [The Devotion to the Sorrowful and Immaculate Heart of Mary] better known to the world by means of notices, leaflets, literature and a wide diffusion of the picture of Our Lady honored at Ollignies.

OUR LADY OF OLLIGNIES

A reproduction of the picture venerated
in the Convent of the Bernardine
Sisters at Ollignies.

9

The picture of Our Lady of Ollignies is of a mysterious origin. It was discovered under peculiar circumstances in 1918 — the year of the Armistice, in the Convent of the Bernardine nuns by whom Berthe had been educated. After the withdrawal of the German troops from Belgium, consequent on the closure of war, one of the sisters was asked to put up the cellar in order. Among the various papers, she found a piece of cardboard wrapped in an old newspaper, which she immediately tore off as useless, to be burnt along with other rubbish; but to her astonishment she found, underneath the cardboard, a beautiful picture of Our Lady. This was reported to the Mother Superior; the whole Community felt that their safety during the war was due to the special protection of Our Lady manifested by that picture within the precincts of the Convent. But, in spite of a thorough investigation, they were never able to trace its origin. When it was shown to Berthe in 1919, after her return from Switzerland, she at once recognized it as the picture of the two-fold symbol of the Sorrowful and Immaculate Heart of Mary.

The image in the picture represents the Mother of God, holding in her left hand a lily, symbol of her Immaculate purity — the gratuitous gift of her Divine Son; the finger of the right hand points out to her Sorrowful Heart surmounted by flames, and pierced with a sword. The faraway gaze of the penetrating eyes seems as if the Blessed Virgin is beholding with sorrow the sins of mankind, which have caused the suffering expressed on the gentle countenance of her head, slightly inclined to the right. The general expression of the face is not quite unlike that of the *"Pieta," so* often seen in our Churches. At first, copies of this picture were distributed with discretion; but soon it came to be widely known and eagerly sought after all over Belgium. It bore *"au verso,"* the Act of Consecration dictated by Our Lord Himself to Berthe Petit, and used by His Eminence Francis Cardinal Bourne, Primate of England, during and after the Great War, and *the Imprimatur* of the Bishop of Tournai. In those war-torn years, when millions were being crushed under the weight of trying sadness, it was but fitting to seek comfort in the Sorrowful and Immaculate Heart of Mary!

ACT OF CONSECRATION

O Lord Jesus, Who on Calvary and in the Holy Eucharist hast shown Thyself to us as God of Love and Mercy, kneeling humbly at Thy feet we adore Thee and beg once more for Thy forgiveness and Thy divine pity. And remembering that, by Thine own act on Calvary, the human race, represented by Thy beloved disciple John, gained a Mother in the Virgin of Sorrows, we desire to honor the sufferings and woes of our Mother's Heart by devoting ourselves to it in solemn Consecration.

It is but just O Mary, that our souls should strive henceforth to venerate thee with special homage under the title of Thy Sorrowful Heart, a title won by sharing in the whole Passion of thy Son and thus co-operating in the work of our redemption -- a title due to thee in justice, and dear, we believe, to Jesus and to thine own Heart, torn by the wound in His.

We consecrate therefore, O Mary, to thy Sorrowful and Immaculate Heart ourselves, our families, our country and those who are fighting for its honor. Have pity on us; see our tribulations, and the anguish of our hearts in the midst of the mourning and calamities that lay waste the world. Deign, O Mother of God, to obtain mercy for us that, being converted and purified by sorrow, and made strong in faith, we may henceforth be devoted servants of Jesus Christ and His Church, for whose triumph we pray. O Mary Immaculate, we promise to be faithful clients of thy Sorrowful Heart. Intercede for us, we beseech thee, with thy Son that, at the cry of thy Sorrowful and Immaculate Heart, His divine Power may speedily bring to pass the triumph of right and justice.

Sacred Heart of Jesus, have pity on us.

Sorrowful and Immaculate Heart of Mary, pray for us and save us.

(This Act of Consecration to the Sorrowful and Immaculate Heart of Mary was made publicly in all the churches of England during World War I, by order of His Eminence, Francis Cardinal Bourne, Primate of England. This was printed at the back of the picture of Our Lady of Ollignies and distributed). Picture on page 44.

PERSONAL CONSECRATION

Composed by Berthe Petit

Sorrowful and Immaculate Heart of Mary, dwelling pure and holy, cover my soul with your maternal protection so that being ever faithful to the voice of Jesus, it responds to His love and obeys His Divine Will.

I wish, O, my Mother, to keep unceasingly before me your co-redemption in order to live intimately with your Heart that is totally united to the Heart of your Divine Son.

Fasten me to this Heart by your own virtues and sorrows. Protect me always.

V. COMPILED MESSAGES ON WWI, WWII AND THE CONSECRATION OF THE WORLD TO THE SORROWFUL AND IMMACULATE HEART OF MARY

On February, 1910 in Alsace, it was revealed to Berthe that her mission would be the *Consecration of the World to the Sorrowful and Immaculate Heart of Mary.*

On September 12, 1912, Our Lord made this announcement to Berthe: "A two-fold murder will strike down the successor of the aged Sovereign, so loyal to the Faith. This will be the first of events, grievous but expedient to My designs, which will precede the chastisement . . ." Later on June 30, 1914, our Lord said to Berthe: "Now begins the onward march of coming events, which are going to lead you to the great showing of My Justice." Concerning the German Emperor, William II, our Lord said, "His ungovernable pride has unleashed a scourge the extent of which cannot be foreseen. He will authorize, in My Name, every kind of ravage, caused in reality, by his own hatred and ambition. But I will break his might and his pride. Heaven will be the reward of the innocent victims and many a soul will turn to Me forever."

"I curse the arrogant people who slight Me and who persecute the true Faith using the while My Name and authority. Any nation that prepares its military forces in advance to hurl them unjustly upon the choicest portion of God's flock, pursuing, albeit for the purification of souls — its ruthless way like a murdering scourge of destruction, is not the nation of My choice. I shall break it and chastise it because, in its insane pride, it refuses to see its own religious and moral decay. It is in the crushing of this pride that My punishment will be manifested." At a later time, Jesus, speaking of the Kaiser, said to Berthe: "I will crush the hypocrite who continues to pose before Me, making it appear that his injustice and cruelty have the seal of My assent."

A little more than four years before the prophecy was realized, He [Jesus] added: "A chastisement will strike down the ambitious one on the very soil he has now unjustly invaded..." On September, 1914, our Lord to his spiritual daughter: "The worst calamities which I had predicted are unleashed.

Later in Aug. 15, 1917, Jesus spoke, "It is I who dispose of life and death. I know the instruments that serve My purpose. You need not, therefore, be disturbed! You must abandon all to My leading. Let no illusion lead you to expect a human victory in the present struggle. The danger remains great for the nations drawn into this fight, and a happy issue can be obtained only through recourse, as I wish it, to the Sorrowful and Immaculate Heart of My Mother." He latter added, "My apostle sees My intervention in the success of the combatants of his nation. He will carry out my wishes faithfully."

Early on the morning of Good Friday, [1918] Jesus appeared to Berthe. He was covered with blood. He said to her: "If My voice had been fully heeded and My orders carried out, I would have put an end this very day to a struggle in which blood is being shed for the sake of an illusive victory. In the midst of so many victims I am reaping an abundant harvest of souls; the prolongation of the trial crushes the vain pride of a great many who were seeking nothing from life but pleasure or who were making their preparations for the persecution of My Church." And later on April 1, 1918, "The days to come will be terrible. There will be enormous losses. How strong and powerful the enemy still is will be plainly seen." "My apostle Francis [Cardinal Bourne] must dispel the pain and agony which he is enduring as a result of the hardships which have fallen upon the combatants of his country; this trial is necessary, for after My protection had enabled them to gain the victory, they attributed the glory of it to their own prowess. Reverses are now showing these soldiers how human means alone are powerless to repel the surge of invasion." And later, "To the consecration of his country to the Sorrowful and Immaculate Heart of My Mother, made by My apostle Francis, according to My orders, he owes My promised intervention from which has resulted the happy issue of the battle in favor of the defenders of his country."

"I should have intervened completely by a remarkable feat which would have led to the lasting peace I desired to give, a peace which would have assured the full victory of My Church, had the other nations acceded to My demand. The combatants have benefited by My protection plain to be seen by those who wish to open their eyes to the light and to acknowledge that it was impossible otherwise to have gained the victory over the enemy. My word has, therefore, been openly brought to pass: 'A chastisement will strike down the ambitious one on the soil invaded,' and that other word: 'I will break his might and his pride.'"

"The hurricane of calamity has not died down and grave dangers from within still threaten all the nations. For many amongst them there remains danger from without. My words will come to pass."

"Let My apostle Francis know that My favorable gaze rests upon him, and his flock. Let him renew with the faithful the solemn consecration to the Sorrowful and Immaculate Heart of My Mother — this time in thanksgiving, for gratitude draws down still more favors. Let him confide to Me entirely his country and the Church of which he is the shepherd, in the way I shall inspire you. Thus will My reign be established firmly in that nation; then more and more souls will open their eyes to the truth; peace and prosperity will reign there, and My Mother, glorified in a fitting manner, will extend to them Her Maternal protection."

"Thus and in this way alone will the internal struggles die down. And I shall scatter blessings upon that nation. My apostle Francis will know the holy joys and consolations of the Shepherds who accomplish My Will."

Later on June 18th, 1918, the Divine Master said to His servant: "The soul of My apostle has fully corresponded with My light, by welcoming this devotion, by drawing attention to it with all the fervor and active zeal which it deserves, and by preparatory prayer disposing hearts for the solemn consecration — source of salvation for souls and source of providential help which will ensure victory."

On the 6th of September, 1918, Jesus made the prophetic revelation which was to be verified only too well by the events which followed the Armistice: "*The leaders of this nation (Germany) who clearly see the peril of invasion with which their country is threatened, are preparing by tactics which no one suspects, and in full agreement with him whom I have pointed out to you as a scheming, hypocritical enemy of My Church, a plan which will temporarily save their nation. In consequence, she will not immediately receive the punishment she deserves.*"

And during the Holy Hour of October 16th, 1918: Our

Lord sent the messenger whom He Himself had chosen in the 17th century to be the apostle of His Sacred Heart — Margaret Mary — to the servant of the Sorrowful and Immaculate Heart of Our Lady, to speak these consoling words:

"Peace be with you, for you are serving a cause so dear to the Sacred Heart. This Divine Heart deigned to turn to me during my earthly pilgrimage which ended without my seeing the glorification of the cause. This was for me a source of sorrow and agonizing suspense which gave me more tribulation than joy. You are fighting, you are suffering for the cause of the Blessed Virgin; and the immensity of the glory, which must flow from its triumph, now entails multiple obstacles which mean trials for your soul."

"But believe in a word which is beyond all doubt. Await its realization, in spite of darkness and anguish. Consider what has already been won for this cause, which the Eternal Son regards as His work of justice and love for His Mother. For you the hour is hard. It is one of struggle, but also of blind confidence which believes and takes for granted the liberty of the divine action in everything."

Turning away her gaze and looking afar, Margaret Mary ended her message saying:

"Poor France is in peril. She is inflated with pride and yet so many hardships will be hurled upon her before the day she is to rise again."

And later Jesus spoke, "Had I not intervened in answer to recourse to the Sorrowful and Immaculate Heart of My Mother, and through the leading of My apostle Francis, victory would have been on the side of those, who long since had set all their energies to prepare and organize a vast scale war to attain their ambitious ends. Material strength would thus have prevailed over justice and right and this more especially so for your own country. For why should I come to the help of the people of a France intent on persecuting My Church, when the leaders should be earnestly organizing resistance to any invader. That is why trials will continue until the day when humbly acknowledging her errors, this nation will render Me My rights and give full liberty to My Church."

"The world is hanging over the edge of the precipice. Confusion will reign increasingly and those who are now singing their victory will see it snatched out of their hands. My

16

Justice does not preside over the intrigues of those who are working in their own interests towards a peace which does not merit the name, and which can never be genuine except through My intervention."

And on November 1918, our Lord spoke, "I have permitted everything, because My wishes for the Heart of My Mother have not been fulfilled"

During July, 1919, Jesus said, : "Internal strife is more rampant than ever in your country. It is being fanned by the evil seed sown by the invader; it is fed by egoism, pride and jealousy — malevolent germs which can only generate moral ruin. I continue to have pity on a country which defended its honor at the cost of the greatest sacrifices, and on a sovereign faithful to his duty. To save this nation, I have wished, and continue to wish, that it should be solemnly consecrated to the Heart of My Mother. People must know that they are consecrated to Her Sorrowful and Immaculate Heart, to the end that they may invoke this Heart; so that in time of danger it may be obvious to all that I have intervened because of this consecration and that My Mother is worthy to be thanked and glorified for ever."

"Time will prove that peace established without Me and without him [i.e., the Holy Father: For the establishment of a just and lasting peace in 1919, Benedict XV was not consulted any more than was Pius XII in 1945] who speaks in My Name, has no stability. The nation which is considered to be vanquished, but whose forces are only momentarily diminished, will remain a menace for your country, and likewise for France. Confusion and terror will steadily spread through every nation."

"Because this peace is not Mine, wars will be rekindled on every side — civil war and racial war. What would have been so noble, so true, so beautiful, so lasting in its fulfillment is consequently delayed . . ."

"Humanity is advancing towards a frightful scourge which will divide the nations more and more; it will reduce human schemes to nothingness; it will break the pride of the powers that be; it will show that nothing subsists without Me and that I remain the only Master of the destinies of nations."

Jesus also deigned to enlighten His servant on the wording of the consecration for the *"post-war"* period. We give it in the form in which it has been spread all over the world:

TEXT OF THE CONSECRATION TO THE SORROWFUL AND IMMACULATE HEART OF MARY

"Lord Jesus, King of kings, many of us never ceased to place full confidence in Your Divine Heart during the long trial of war. Many, likewise, have implored the help of Your Mother, and we wish to show our gratitude by consecrating ourselves to Her Sorrowful and Immaculate Heart."

"It is fitting that we should honor this Sorrowful Heart by special veneration. For Your Mother, O Lord, acquired this title when She shared Your Passion and thus co-operated in the work of our Redemption; a just title which we believe to be dear to Your Heart, and to Her Heart pierced with the wound of Yours."

"We, therefore, O Blessed Mother, consecrate to Your Sorrowful and Immaculate Heart, our persons, our families and our country. We beseech You to come to our help as a Mother."

"Behold the trials that oppress us, the menace of evil and the dangers that surround us. We beseech You to obtain for us from Your Divine Son, solace in suffering, social unity between classes and the preservation of peace."

"May the reign of the Sacred Heart, a reign of justice and love, be extended throughout our dear country, and may Your Sorrowful and Immaculate Heart, loved and invoked, reign over us also, O Blessed Mother, and ever obtain for us the mercy and blessing of God."

On March, 1921, Jesus again spoke, "The ravening nation desirous of a prompt revenge is preparing a destructive mechanism which will soon be ready. Then, rapidly and with her thorough organization she will swoop down upon those whom she would lay low."

And later in June of that same year, our Lord spoke these words: "Events are unleashed in Italy. Their work of destruction is but a feeble image of the punishment which will strike this nation, which is to be deceived in the evil day by motives cleverly veiled." And on another day: "When he of whom I have spoken to you will be struck down, the cataclysm will be at hand."

18

On October 24, 1921: It was Our Lady who spoke thus: "Events are nearing, like an ever growing shadow imperceptibly widening, and all the while concealing frightful sparks which will plunge the nations once again into fire and blood. Oh! What a terrifying thought! My maternal Heart would be broken, did I not know that divine Justice is intervening for the salvation of souls and the cleansing of nations . . ."

On February 6, 1922, Jesus once again said: "My apostle will arise at the appointed hour when the horrible cataclysm, which is coming, will have overthrown the machinations of men and their deplorable state-craft. It is not at the present time that My wish concerning the glory of My Mother will be accomplished. A period of waiting is still necessary for the work to grow in greatness." And later in September of that same year, Our Lady gave to his spiritual child: "My daughter, let your souls bless my Son for the choice He has made of you in the accomplishment of His express wish. Events have occurred, preparations are made which are the unassailable foundations for the cause which you serve. The work will attain its end and this with the amplitude willed by God. The way which leads to this result is arid, devoid of repose, at times even painful for your souls, as you labor to comply with my requests. But have confidence: strife will come to an end and my Son will triumph. See how humanity is crushed by sorrow, while evil is diabolically making progress. There have been catastrophes; there will be more. But what are they? Merely a beginning, a feeble image of the dreadful calamities predicted to you by my Son!. . ."

"Persevere in your task by complete forgetfulness of yourselves, and by the one only thought of obeying my Son for the realization of His designs. My Heart, full of pity for humanity, bows down before divine Justice which is on the way to manifesting itself on a magnificent scale. Each nation is preparing its own punishment: some are actuated by their rapacity, others by their ambitions, while others again refuse to put an end to the ravages of passion. As for you, our servants, look with confidence to a future guided by infinite Wisdom, Mercy and Power."

And on February 11th, 1924, what follows is the Words of Our Lord concerning Italy and its Duce:

"Those who allow themselves to be dominated by pride and who are guided by ambition, will not escape My justice. The present government of that nation is motivated by its passions. That government which has the semblance of giving promise of a better era, will collapse in disillusionment. The man you have named is veiling his ambition under the guise of benevolence to the Church. This is but one more ruse planned by the ungodly sect to attain the end towards which its efforts are directed, by lulling to sleep all uneasiness." And later on September 24th of the same year: "All the nations are heading towards a frightful cataclysm. I alone can appease the hatred and the discord, and hasten the reign of peace. I shall do it when My wishes for the Heart of My Mother will be accomplished. It will come to pass when the hour of despair will strike — an hour towards which everything is moving. Then, in response to the supplications which will ascend to the Sorrowful and Immaculate Heart of My Mother, I will manifest My power by a miraculous intervention which will impress everyone. The whole of Christendom will bow before this triumph which I, as Son, have determined for My Mother. Tell My apostle that this Sorrowful Heart must be more and more his dwelling."

A message from our Lord in 1928: "If men could see the frightful means of destruction and if they would reflect on what is being prepared for a future war of revenge, there is no one who would not wish to die! Belgium, dangerously menaced, is more in peril than she realizes: she will be saved neither by her prudence, nor by her strength. She will not secure any triumph against her enemies. She can defend herself only with help from Heaven. She has no other refuge than the arms of God. He will open His divine arms at the prayer of His Mother, the Virgin Mary, and on condition that this Kingdom be consecrated to the Sorrowful and Immaculate Heart of the Mother of God and of men."

On Good Friday, 1931, Jesus spoke: "The world is inundated with crime, and there are the sins of priests, and the scandal of immodest fashions. The evils that will break upon the world will be frightful."

Later on April 27th, 1934, our Lord told her: "The storm is abating. So many prayers are ascending to me! So many supplications, sincere and ardent, are being sent up to My Heart and through that of My Mother, that I will impose on the mighty one an era of peace, of short duration however, because the spirit of evil does not cease to incite and to goad the pride of any nation which lives only on the thought of revenge and domination."

And on September 1st, 1939 [The invasion of Poland by Germany], Jesus stated: "That nation is on the way to its own undoing. It is responsible for its illusory pride." And on January 22, 1940, the following words rang in her ears like a death-knell: "Belgium will be invaded."

Then on November 4, 1941, Jesus spoke, "The invader is at My Mercy for the punishment he deserves. Justice will be done in everything. The chastisement is rumbling, the leaders feel it coming near, they dread it and they realize that they can do nothing to avert it. It is then that My judgment and the power of My Will shall be made known. My Work will never fall short of achievement. Belgium will again be prosperous." And later on in December of that same year, Jesus states: "The safety of your country, internal peace and confidence in My Church will revive through the spread of the Devotion and the Consecration which I wish in order that the Sorrowful and Immaculate Heart of My Mother, united in all to My Heart, may be loved and glorified. Deliverance will thus be the work of our two Hearts, the triumph of our love for the people upon whom this Consecration will bestow confidence according to My promises."

And on April 25th 1942: Our Lord, making allusion to the increasing tempo of the war, said: "A frightful torment is in preparation. It will be seen that the forces launched with such fury, will soon be let loose. It is, now or never, the moment for all of you to give yourselves to the Sorrowful and Immaculate Heart of My Mother. By her acceptance of Calvary My Mother has participated in all My sufferings. Devotion to her Heart united to Mine will bring peace, that true peace, so often implored and yet so little merited."

VI. CHRONOLOGICAL LIST OF MESSAGES TO BERTHE PETIT

Circa 1874: . . . she [Berthe] beheld the tabernacle open wide and the Infant Jesus coming towards her. Signing her forehead, He said: "You will always suffer, but I shall be with you."

On Christmas Night, 1893: Jesus said to Berthe: "Thy sacrifice has been accepted, thy petition granted. Behold thy Priest: thou wilt know him one day. . . . Magdalen, I accept thy donation. . . Thou shalt be a victim! . . . Thy life is for him, thy sufferings have saved him. . . Here is the cross which I offer thee. It is heavy, but I shall bear it with thee!"

On the 14th of May, 1907 at Lourdes: Our Lady spoke to her [Berthe] thus on arrival at the Grotto: "My Son loves His crucified spouse. We both love you. You will know the member of the priesthood who has responded to your sacrifice."

On the 16th May, 1907 at Lourdes: Our Blessed Lady said to her: "Love your sufferings; they console My Son. You will suffer always."

In May, 1907 as Berthe was leaving Lourdes: The Immaculate Mother added: "Come back again, my child, I will help you."

In 1908 at Lourdes: Mary confirmed her promise: "You will see the priest whom you begged from God, twenty years ago, and the meeting is close at hand."

On September 4th, 1908: Christ encouraged her [Berthe] in these words: "Your sufferings have won, and will continue to win, an abundance of graces. Be always a ready victim! Accept with more courage the cross of life! You can still help the priest whom you are soon to know."

In 1908 at Paris: Our Lord said to her: "I wish to gratify your long waiting, because of your suffering in which your only desire was to accomplish My Divine Will: you shall meet your priest."

In 1908: Jesus revealed Himself to His servant, and she heard these words: "This is the priest for whom I have accepted your sacrifice; My mother and I bless you." Our Lady said to her: "What my Son desired is being accomplished."

In 1908: The Savior said to Berthe: "Be faithful to My grace: My work will be accomplished."

The Midnight Mass of Christmas 1909: "Teach souls to love the Heart of My Mother pierced by the very sorrows which pierced Mine."

On February 7, 1910: "You must contemplate the Heart of My Mother, as you contemplate My own; live in that Heart as you wish to live in Mine; give yourself to that Heart as you give yourself to Mine; spread the love of Her Heart which is wholly united to Mine."

On February 8, 1910: "I have made known to you the wishes of My Heart concerning the Devotion to the Heart of My Mother. Love it and make it loved! This love will be for you and for the whole world a source of grace, and it will bring upon you great blessings. Surrender yourself to My love. The pressing desire of My Heart is about to be confided to you . . ."

On February, 1910 in Alsace: It was revealed to Berthe that her mission would be the *Consecration of the World to the Sorrowful and Immaculate Heart of Mary.*

On February, 1910 in Alsace: Placing on Berthe's head a crown of thorns, Saint [Catherine] said to her: "Wear this as I did! . . . It is the wish of Divine Love. Obey: this Love wills that I protect you."

1910: Jesus said: "The soul of my servant [Father] Albert

[Condamin] is very dear to Me."

On 1910: Our Lord said words: "The world must be consecrated to the Sorrowful and Immaculate Heart of My Mother as it is to Mine. Fear nothing, no matter what obstacle or suffering you may encounter; your only object must be the accomplishment of My Will."

On 1910 Easter Sunday: The Hearts of Jesus and Mary, closely united and surmounted by a dove, appeared once again to Berthe and she heard the following words: "This wish of Mine follows from what I accomplished on Calvary. When I gave John to My Mother as her son, did I not confide the whole world to Her Sorrowful and Immaculate Heart?" Then the Savior ordered her to make a sketch of the vision of the two Hearts. "I shall guide your hand," He said. In obedience to this command Berthe reproduced what she had seen — the sketch which is given below:

On June 3rd 1910: "It is My desire that this picture, guided by My hand, be spread far and wide, simultaneously with the invocation. Wherever it will be venerated, My Mercy and My Love will be made manifest and the sight of Our Hearts, wounded by the same wound, will encourage tepid and weak souls to come back to their duty."

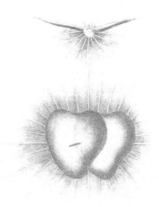

Sketch of the Vision of the Two Hearts

On September 17th 1910: "Saint Catherine of Siena appeared once again to Berthe and said: "Jesus confided a mission to me. To further it I endured many a painful hour. I have known mockery and contempt: I have seen incredulity deny the divine workings. You have been chosen for another mission which will meet with every kind of obstacle, but which will triumph later, for the Master wills it. Be resigned to everything and have unfailing confidence."

Circa 1910?: "I am thy real nourishment," He [Jesus] said to her at the beginning of her fast, when He forbade her [Berthe] to make any further vain efforts to take solid food.

At Loreto in 1910: He [Jesus] insisted in this wise: "Do you know that I, and nought beside, am your life?"

On June 17th 1911: Mary appeared again to Her servant. . . and said: "See here the wound of My Heart, similar to that of my Son, and the torrent of grace ready to gush forth from it . . . . "Do not allow any trial, any disappointment, any suffering to discourage you."

On September 8th 1911: "The Heart of My Mother has the right to be called *Sorrowful* and I wish this title placed *before* that of *Immaculate* because She has won it Herself. The Church has defined in the case of My Mother what I Myself had ordained — Her Immaculate Conception. This right which My Mother has to a title of justice, is now, according to My express wish, to be known and universally accepted. She has earned it by Her identification with My sorrows, by Her sufferings: by Her sacrifices and Her immolation on Calvary endured in perfect correspondence with My grace for the salvation of mankind."

"In Her co-redemption lies the nobility of My Mother and for this reason I ask that the Invocation which I have demanded be approved and spread through the whole Church. It has already obtained many graces; it will obtain yet more when the Church will be exalted and the world renewed through its Consecration to the Sorrowful and Immaculate Heart of My Mother."

On September 17th 1911: On September 17th, Our Lady appeared again, her brow wounded and bleeding, her hands and Heart pierced. By those sacred stigmata, Mary showed how much She identified Herself with the sufferings of Jesus; and while the servant of God was, more than ever, interiorly enlightened on this Compassion, Mary said: "You can now understand the sorrows which my Heart endured, the sufferings of my whole being for the salvation of the world."

On the 24th to the 25th of March, 1912, Mary deigned to add: "I have called myself the Immaculate Conception. To you I call myself Mother of the Sorrowful Heart. This title willed by my Son is dear to me above all others. According as it is spread everywhere, there will be granted graces of mercy, spiritual renewal and salvation."

On the 2nd of April, 1912: On the Feast of St. Joseph (that year transferred to April 2nd) Our Lord said to her: "Joseph, who supported My Mother and protected My divine Infancy, is your support in a cause which is so dear to him, because he knew many of the sorrows which transfixed My Mother's Heart, and he foresaw, before his death, all that Her Heart would still have to endure."

September 12, 1912: Our Lord made this announcement to Berthe: "A two-fold murder will strike down the successor of the aged Sovereign, so loyal to the Faith. This will be the first of events, grievous but expedient to My designs, which will precede the chastisement . . ."

In 1913: Jesus said again of him [Father Albert Condamin]: "He is an untiring worker." And when told of this praise, the priest was astonished. Jesus said once more: "It is not because of the work of intelligence, or devotedness, or religious activity that I estimate in My divine mind either labor, or prayer, or renunciation. I perceive the motives that animate minds and hearts and my gaze rests there where I find true zeal for the good of souls, childlike humility and sincere renouncement. "Untiring" he is, therefore, who ceases not to seek Me in everything. This is what pleases My Heart. This is what attracts My glance of love."

In 1913: "The hour has come for My servant Albert [Condamin] who, as you know, is specially loved by My Heart and by that of My Mother, to aid in the work I have entrusted to you, by becoming the zealous apostle of the Sorrowful and Immaculate Heart of My Mother which has won for itself the gaze of My merciful Love. Blessings will follow the apostolate of my chosen servant, and every light will be given him for his co-operation. He will communicate the writings of your director to My apostle Francis ("the chief Bishop of England?" asked Berthe — "Yes," replied Jesus), whom I bless, and he will ardently plead before the Prelate the cause of the Sorrowful and Immaculate Heart of My Mother. Let My apostle Francis thus enlightened, adopt the devotion and promulgate it."

"Let him grant to the invocation "Sorrowful and Immaculate Heart of Mary, pray for us" the privilege it already has (100 days indulgence granted in 1911 by Cardinal Mercier). Let him propagate the devotion through the voice of his priests, so that souls may be duly prepared for the solemn consecration of their country to the Sorrowful and Immaculate Heart of My Mother. When he has fulfilled this, my apostle Francis will see My protection extended to his flock, his country and eventually the triumph of justice."

"As I have done in the case of your country and of France, I offer to this nation the providential help of My merciful Heart."

1914: During the Holy Hour, Our Lady appeared to the patient and reassured her saying: "You have only to have recourse to me for help."

June 30, 1914: Our Lord said to Berthe: "Now begins the onward march of coming events, which are going to lead you to the great showing of My Justice."

July 29, 1914, concerning the German Emperor, William II: "His ungovernable pride has unleashed a scourge the extent of which cannot be foreseen. He will authorize, in My Name, every kind of ravage, caused in reality, by his own hatred and ambition. But I will break his might and his pride. Heaven will be the reward of the innocent victims and many a soul will turn to Me forever . . ."

August 6th, 1914: "I curse the arrogant people who slight Me and who persecute the true Faith using the while My Name and authority. Any nation that prepares its military forces in advance to hurl them unjustly upon the choicest portion of God's flock, pursuing, albeit for the purification of souls — its ruthless way like a murdering scourge of destruction, is not the nation of My choice. I shall break it and chastise it because, in its insane pride, it refuses to see its own religious and moral decay. It is in the crushing of this pride that My punishment will be manifested."

September 3rd, 1914: At this time, Jesus, speaking of the Kaiser, said to Berthe: "I will crush the hypocrite who continues to pose before Me, making it appear that his injustice and cruelty have the seal of My assent."

10th of September, 1914: a little more than four years before the prophecy was realized, He [Jesus] added: "A chastisement will strike down the ambitious one on the very soil he has now unjustly invaded . . ."

September, 1914: Our Lord to his spiritual daughter: "The worst calamities which I had predicted are unleashed. The time is now ripe and I wish mankind to turn to the Sorrowful and Immaculate Heart of My Mother. Let this prayer be uttered by every soul: *'Sorrowful and Immaculate Heart of Mary, pray for us.'* Let this prayer dictated by My Love as a supreme succor be approved and indulgenced, no longer partially and for a small portion of My flock, but for the whole universe, so that it may spread as a refreshing and purifying balm of reparation that will appease My anger."

"This Devotion to the Sorrowful and Immaculate Heart of My Mother will restore faith and hope to broken hearts and to ruined families: it will help to repair the destruction: it will sweeten sorrow. It will be a new strength for My Church, bringing souls, not only to confidence in My Heart, but also to abandonment to the Sorrowful Heart of My Mother."

September, 1914: it was Our Lady who appeared before

Berthe to tell her: "It is with an unshakable resolve that my Son wills souls to have recourse to my Sorrowful Heart. With my heart overflowing with tenderness, I am awaiting this gesture on the part of souls, that I may reiterate to the Heart of my Son whatever will be confided to my own Heart, and thus obtain graces of salvation for all."

December 13th, 1914: That same day as Berthe was leaving the Collegiate Church where she had prayed for the cause so dear to her heart, she heard a voice hissing with fury: "I will wage war against you to the end, by obsessing minds, hardening hearts and feeding passions!"

December 14th, 1914: "Bear all for the cause and for your country," said the Divine Master with unutterable sweetness during her Holy Communion next morning. No doubt, she was paying already for the great joy which awaited her at the end of the month of May, 1915 . . .

February, 1916: "It is through the Sorrowful and Immaculate Heart of My Mother that I will triumph, because having co-operated in the redemption of souls, this Heart has the right to share a similar co-operation in the manifestations of My justice and of My love. My Mother is noble in everything, but She is especially so in Her wounded Heart, transfixed by the wound of Mine."

"Desiring for Her Heart a radiant, dazzling, brilliant triumph, I have awaited this time of universal distress which finds an echo in the Sorrowful Heart of My Mother, a Heart universal as My own. To adopt this Devotion and to spread it, is to accomplish My Will and to respond to the wishes of My Heart. Because, by prayer and by the consecration made to this Heart, graces of light will be obtained. They will gradually bring souls to the full knowledge of our united Hearts, which have been wounded by the same wound, the inexhaustible source of all good for humanity, and the glory of which is now, and ever will be, the happiness of the elect for Eternity."

March, 1916: Our Lord said to Berthe: "To you I assign My Mother as supreme Mediatrix through Her Sorrowful Heart."

March 30, 1916: Jesus said to her: "In your mission of making known the Sorrowful and Immaculate Heart of My Mother, your fasting has not been the essential point in proof of the timeliness of the Devotion or the justice of the title for which I wish a foremost place when appeal is made to my intervention. I wished to be your sole nourishment. For My Love has so ordained it: My Providence so designed it."

September, 1916: Jesus . . . dictated to her the following prayer:

ACT OF CONSECRATION TO THE SORROWFUL AND IMMACULATE HEART OF MARY

"O Lord Jesus Who, on Calvary and in the Holy Eucharist, hast shown Thyself to us as the God of love and mercy, kneeling humbly at Thy feet we adore Thee and beg once more for Thy forgiveness and for Thy divine pity on the third year of this unexampled war."

"And remembering that, by Thine own act on Calvary, the human race, represented by Thy beloved disciple John, gained a Mother in the Virgin of Sorrows, we desire to honor the sufferings and woes of our Mother's Heart by devoting ourselves to it in solemn consecration."

"It is but just, O Mary, that our souls should strive henceforth to venerate thee with special homage under the title of thy Sorrowful Heart — a title won by sharing in the whole Passion of thy divine Son and thus co-operating in the work of our redemption — a title due to thee in justice, and dear, we believe, to Jesus, and to thine own Heart wounded by the wound in His."

"We consecrate, therefore, O Mary, to thy Sorrowful and Immaculate Heart, ourselves, our families, our country, and those who are fighting for its honor. Have pity upon us; see our tribulations, and the anguish of our hearts in the midst of the mourning and calamities that lay waste the world. Deign, O Mother of God, to obtain mercy for us that, being converted and purified by sorrow, and made strong in faith, we may henceforth be devoted servants of Jesus Christ and of His Church, for whose triumph we pray. O Mary Immaculate, we promise to be faithful clients of thy Sorrowful Heart. Intercede

30

for us, we beseech thee, with thy Son that, at the very cry of thy Sorrowful and Immaculate Heart, His divine Power may speedily bring to pass the triumph of right and justice."

"Sacred Heart of Jesus, have pity upon us."

"Sorrowful and Immaculate Heart of Mary, pray for us and save us."

March 30th, 1917: "I wish," said Our Lord at this time to Berthe, "that My apostle Francis (Cardinal Bourne) make the Solemn Consecration of his country on the Feast commemorating the day when, as the fruit of the joyful and the sorrowful 'Fiat' of My Mother, I appeared in the world as the Savior of the human race (Christmas, therefore)."

June 30th, 1917: "On this Feast of My Heart, a twofold Feast in Heaven where reign our united Hearts, abundant blessings are being poured upon My apostle Francis, and upon all those who, thanks to this exhortation, are already invoking the Heart of My Mother in accordance with the formula which I have dictated. By a solemn consecration to the Sorrowful and Immaculate Heart of My Mother, he will soon deliver his country, the Church and the flock confided to him. I shall give ear to his pious aspirations. He will see, too, My divine intervention in all his anxieties. But I wish him to abandon all to Me with full confidence in the light which will guide him ever for the greater good and the triumph of My Church. My Mother, touched by this act of My apostle in honor of Her Heart, is giving him Her maternal protection, he will have the proof of this in the most consoling way when My Will is fully accomplished."

Aug 22nd, 1917: "I ask My apostle Francis [Cardinal Bourne] to exert an ever increasing activity in favor of the Sorrowful and Immaculate Heart of My Mother — an activity which will be reflected in the zealous preaching of His clergy, so that souls may turn in prayerful confidence to the Heart of My Mother. Soon My apostle will feel, personally, that the devotion will bring help in the hour of need, and eventual salvation to many souls."

"Let him hasten what he calls his 'first step' so that a still more solemn consecration may be timed for the Feast of the

Dolors of My Mother — the great Feast of Her Heart as Co-Redemptrix."

"When the nation of My apostle Francis will be entirely dedicated to this Heart he will see that he has not listened to My word in vain, for My providential intervention is reserved for all the people consecrated to the Sorrowful and Immaculate Heart of My Mother. I wish thus to show the power of this Heart which is united in everything with My own."

"My apostle Francis will also see the increasing support of Benedict XV for this devotion to the Sorrows of the Heart of My Mother till the day when — the devotion having triumphed in the nations of My choice by reason of the zeal of their apostles — the glory of our united Hearts will extend everywhere for the salvation of souls."

Aug. 15, 1917: "It is I who dispose of life and death. I know the instruments that serve My purpose. You need not, therefore, be disturbed! You must abandon all to My leading. Let no illusion lead you to expect a human victory in the present struggle. The danger remains great for the nations drawn into this fight, and a happy issue can be obtained only through recourse, as I wish it, to the Sorrowful and Immaculate Heart of My Mother."

On December 24th, 1917: "My apostle sees My intervention in the success of the combatants of his nation. He will carry out my wishes faithfully."

March 29th, 1918: Early on the morning of Good Friday, Jesus appeared to Berthe. He was covered with blood. He said to her: "If My voice had been fully heeded and My orders carried out, I would have put an end this very day to a struggle in which blood is being shed for the sake of an illusive victory. In the midst of so many victims I am reaping an abundant harvest of souls; the prolongation of the trial crushes the vain pride of a great many who were seeking nothing from life but pleasure or who were making their preparations for the persecution of My Church."

April 1, 1918: "The days to come will be terrible. There will be enormous losses. How strong and powerful the enemy still is will be plainly seen."

April 26, 1918: "My apostle Francis [Cardinal Bourne] must dispel the pain and agony which he is enduring as a result of the hardships which have fallen upon the combatants of his country; this trial is necessary, for after My protection had enabled them to gain the victory, they attributed the glory of it to their own prowess. Reverses are now showing these soldiers how human means alone are powerless to repel the surge of invasion."

April 30th, 1918: "To the consecration of his country to the Sorrowful and Immaculate Heart of My Mother, made by My apostle Francis, according to My orders, he owes My promised intervention from which has resulted the happy issue of the battle in favor of the defenders of his country."

"I should have intervened completely by a remarkable feat which would have led to the lasting peace I desired to give, a peace which would have assured the full victory of My Church, had the other nations acceded to My demand. The combatants have benefited by My protection plain to be seen by those who wish to open their eyes to the light and to acknowledge that it was impossible otherwise to have gained the victory over the enemy. My word has, therefore, been openly brought to pass: 'A chastisement will strike down the ambitious one on the soil invaded,' and that other word: 'I will break his might and his pride.' "

"The hurricane of calamity has not died down and grave dangers from within still threaten all the nations. For many amongst them there remains danger from without. My words will come to pass."

"Let My apostle Francis know that My favorable gaze rests upon him, and his flock. Let him renew with the faithful the solemn consecration to the Sorrowful and Immaculate Heart of My Mother — this time in thanksgiving, for gratitude draws down still more favors. Let him confide to Me entirely his country and the Church of which he is the shepherd, in the way I shall inspire you. Thus will My reign be established firmly in that nation; then more and more souls will open their eyes to the truth; peace and prosperity will reign there, and My Mother, glorified in a fitting manner, will extend to them Her Maternal protection."

"Thus and in this way alone will the internal struggles die down. And I shall scatter blessings upon that nation. My apostle Francis will know the holy joys and consolations of the Shepherds who accomplish My Will."

June 18th, 1918: The Divine Master said to His servant: "The soul of My apostle has fully corresponded with My light, by welcoming this devotion, by drawing attention to it with all the fervor and active zeal which it deserves, and by preparatory prayer disposing hearts for the solemn consecration — source of salvation for souls and source of providential help which will ensure victory."

6th of September, 1918: Jesus made the prophetic revelation which was to be verified only too well by the events which followed the Armistice: *"The leaders of this nation (Germany) who clearly see the peril of invasion with which their country is threatened, are preparing by tactics which no one suspects, and in full agreement with him whom I have pointed out to you as a scheming, hypocritical enemy of My Church, a plan which will temporarily save their nation. In consequence, she will not immediately receive the punishment she deserves."*

During the Holy Hour of October 16th, 1918: Our Lord sent the messenger whom He Himself had chosen in the 17th century to be the apostle of His Sacred Heart — Margaret Mary — to the servant of the Sorrowful and Immaculate Heart of Our Lady, to speak these consoling words:

"Peace be with you, for you are serving a cause so dear to the Sacred Heart. This Divine Heart deigned to turn to me during my earthly pilgrimage which ended without my seeing the glorification of the cause. This was for me a source of sorrow and agonizing suspense which gave me more tribulation than joy. You are fighting, you are suffering for the cause of the Blessed Virgin; and the immensity of the glory, which must flow from its triumph, now entails multiple obstacles which mean trials for your soul."

"But believe in a word which is beyond all doubt. Await its realization, in spite of darkness and anguish. Consider what has already been won for this cause, which the Eternal Son regards as His work of justice and love for His Mother. For you the hour is hard. It is one of struggle, but also of blind confidence which believes and takes for granted the liberty of the divine action in everything."

Turning away her gaze and looking afar, Margaret Mary ended her message saying:

"Poor France is in peril. She is inflated with pride and yet so many hardships will be hurled upon her before the day she is to rise again."

October 17th, 1918: "Had I not intervened in answer to recourse to the Sorrowful and Immaculate Heart of My Mother, and through the leading of My apostle Francis, victory would have been on the side of those, who long since had set all their energies to prepare and organize a vast scale war to attain their ambitious ends. Material strength would thus have prevailed over justice and right and this more especially so for your own country. For why should I come to the help of the people of a France intent on persecuting My Church, when the leaders should be earnestly organizing resistance to any invader. That is why trials will continue until the day when humbly acknowledging her errors, this nation will render Me My rights and give full liberty to My Church."

October 28th, 1918: "The world is hanging over the edge of the precipice. Confusion will reign increasingly and those who are now singing their victory will see it snatched out of their hands. My Justice does not preside over the intrigues of those who are working in their own interests towards a peace which does not merit the name, and which can never be genuine except through My intervention."

November 1918: "I have permitted everything, because My wishes for the Heart of My Mother have not been fulfilled"

In July, 1919: "Internal strife is more rampant than ever in your country. It is being fanned by the evil seed sown by the invader; it is fed by egoism, pride and jealousy — malevolent germs which can only generate moral ruin. I continue to have pity on a country which defended its honor at the cost of the greatest sacrifices, and on a sovereign faithful to his duty.

To save this nation, I have wished, and continue to wish, that it should be solemnly consecrated to the Heart of My Mother. People must know that they are consecrated to Her Sorrowful and Immaculate Heart, to the end that they may invoke this Heart; so that in time of danger it may be obvious to all that I have intervened because of this consecration and that My Mother is worthy to be thanked and glorified for ever."

"Time will prove that peace established without Me and without him [i.e., the Holy Father: For the establishment of a just and lasting peace in 1919, Benedict XV was not consulted any more than was Pius XII in 1945] who speaks in My Name, has no stability. The nation which is considered to be vanquished, but whose forces are only momentarily diminished, will remain a menace for your country, and likewise for France. Confusion and terror will steadily spread through every nation."

"Because this peace is not Mine, wars will be rekindled on every side — civil war and racial war. What would have been so noble, so true, so beautiful, so lasting in its fulfillment is consequently delayed . . ."

"Humanity is advancing towards a frightful scourge which will divide the nations more and more; it will reduce human schemes to nothingness; it will break the pride of the powers that be; it will show that nothing subsists without Me and that I remain the only Master of the destinies of nations."

Jesus also deigned to enlighten His servant on the wording of the consecration for the "*post-war*" period. We give it in the form in which it has been spread all over the world:

TEXT OF THE CONSECRATION TO THE SORROWFUL AND IMMACULATE HEART OF MARY

"Lord Jesus, King of kings, many of us never ceased to place full confidence in Your Divine Heart during the long trial of war. Many, likewise, have implored the help of Your Mother, and we wish to show our gratitude by consecrating ourselves to Her Sorrowful and Immaculate Heart."

"It is fitting that we should honor this Sorrowful Heart by special veneration. For Your Mother, O Lord, acquired this title when She shared Your Passion and thus co-operated in the work of our Redemption; a just title which we believe to be dear to Your Heart, and to Her Heart pierced with the wound of Yours."

"We, therefore, O Blessed Mother, consecrate to Your Sorrowful and Immaculate Heart, our persons, our families and our country. We beseech You to come to our help as a Mother."

"Behold the trials that oppress us, the menace of evil and the dangers that surround us. We beseech You to obtain for us from Your Divine Son, solace in suffering, social unity between classes and the preservation of peace."

"May the reign of the Sacred Heart, a reign of justice and love, be extended throughout our dear country, and may Your Sorrowful and Immaculate Heart, loved and invoked, reign over us also, O Blessed Mother, and ever obtain for us the mercy and blessing of God."

October, 1920: "The title of Immaculate belongs to the whole being of My Mother and not specially to Her Heart. This title flows from my gratuitous gift to the Virgin who was to give me birth. My Mother has acquired for her Heart the title of Sorrowful by sharing generously in all the sufferings of My Heart and My Body from the crib to the cross. There is not one of these Sorrows which did not pierce the Heart of My Mother. Living image of My crucified Body, her virginal flesh bore the invisible marks of My wounds as her Heart felt the Sorrows of My own. Nothing could ever tarnish the incorruptibility of her Immaculate Heart."

"The title of 'Sorrowful' belongs therefore to the Heart of My Mother, and more than any other, this title is dear to Her because it springs from the union of her Heart with Mine in the redemption of humanity. This title has been acquired by her through her full participation in My Calvary, and it precedes the gratuitous title 'Immaculate' which My love bestowed upon her by a singular privilege."

March, 1921: "The ravening nation desirous of a prompt revenge is preparing a destructive mechanism which will soon be ready. Then, rapidly and with her thorough organization she will swoop down upon those whom she would lay low."

June 21, 1921: "Events are unleashed in Italy. Their

work of destruction is but a feeble image of the punishment which will strike this nation, which is to be deceived in the evil day by motives cleverly veiled." And on another day: "When he of whom I have spoken to you will be struck down, the cataclysm will be at hand."

October 24, 1921: It was Our Lady who spoke thus: "Events are nearing, like an ever growing shadow imperceptibly widening, and all the while concealing frightful sparks which will plunge the nations once again into fire and blood. Oh! What a terrifying thought! My maternal Heart would be broken, did I not know that divine Justice is intervening for the salvation of souls and the cleansing of nations . . ."

February 6, 1922: "My apostle will arise at the appointed hour when the horrible cataclysm, which is coming, will have overthrown the machinations of men and their deplorable state-craft. It is not at the present time that My wish concerning the glory of My Mother will be accomplished. A period of waiting is still necessary for the work to grow in greatness."

September 29, 1922: Our Lady gave to his spiritual child: "My daughter, let your souls bless my Son for the choice He has made of you in the accomplishment of His express wish. Events have occurred, preparations are made which are the unassailable foundations for the cause which you serve. The work will attain its end and this with the amplitude willed by God. The way which leads to this result is arid, devoid of repose, at times even painful for your souls, as you labor to comply with my requests. But have confidence: strife will come to an end and my Son will triumph. See how humanity is crushed by sorrow, while evil is diabolically making progress. There have been catastrophes; there will be more. But what are they? Merely a beginning, a feeble image of the dreadful calamities predicted to you by my Son!. . ."

"Persevere in your task by complete forgetfulness of yourselves, and by the one only thought of obeying my Son for the realization of His designs. My Heart, full of pity for humanity, bows down before divine Justice which is on the way to manifesting itself on a magnificent scale. Each nation is preparing its own punishment: some are actuated by their rapacity, others by their ambitions, while others again refuse to put an end to the ravages of passion. As for you, our servants, look with confidence to a future guided by infinite Wisdom, Mercy and Power."

October 1923: The Divine Master said to her during thanksgiving: "Your trial is painful to your customary activity. It could have happened to others, but I choose my victims according to the amount of suffering they are willing to accept and to their complete abandonment, leaving Me free to use it as I desire. The trial is meritorious in the measure in which it is hard and crucifying to nature. It can neither surprise nor discourage those who know that I am the supreme Master!"

October 20th, 1923: Our Lady came in her turn: "Your trial would have had fatal consequences if it had not been expressly permitted. You are broken and bruised; there will remain painful scars, but I shall cure you when the amount of suffering needed by my Divine Son will be attained. I am leaving succor which will help you bear your pain."

October 24th, 1923: "I shall complete your cure, but I am leaving the marks of your fall which, humanly speaking, would have been fatal. You require strength to continue the great task indicated by my Son, Who is prolonging your life in accordance with His designs."

February 11th, 1924: Words of Our Lord concerning Italy and its Duce:
"Those who allow themselves to be dominated by pride and who are guided by ambition, will not escape My justice. The present government of that nation is motivated by its passions. That government which has the semblance of giving promise of a better era, will collapse in disillusionment. The man you have named is veiling his ambition under the guise of benevolence to the Church. This is but one more ruse planned by the ungodly sect to attain the end towards which its efforts are directed, by lulling to sleep all uneasiness."

March 19th, 1924: Saint Joseph appeared several times to the servant of God [Berthe Petit], notably on March 19,

1924, with the object of encouraging the Cardinal to devote himself to the Devotion dear to the Mother of God.

September 24ᵗʰ, 1924: "All the nations are heading towards a frightful cataclysm. I alone can appease the hatred and the discord, and hasten the reign of peace. I shall do it when My wishes for the Heart of My Mother will be accomplished. It will come to pass when the hour of despair will strike — an hour towards which everything is moving. Then, in response to the supplications which will ascend to the Sorrowful and Immaculate Heart of My Mother, I will manifest My power by a miraculous intervention which will impress everyone. The whole of Christendom will bow before this triumph which I, as Son, have determined for My Mother. Tell My apostle that this Sorrowful Heart must be more and more his dwelling."

In 1928: "If men could see the frightful means of destruction and if they would reflect on what is being prepared for a future war of revenge, there is no one who would not wish to die! Belgium, dangerously menaced, is more in peril than she realizes: she will be saved neither by her prudence, nor by her strength. She will not secure any triumph against her enemies. She can defend herself only with help from Heaven. She has no other refuge than the arms of God. He will open His divine arms at the prayer of His Mother, the Virgin Mary, and on condition that this Kingdom be consecrated to the Sorrowful and Immaculate Heart of the Mother of God and of men."

December 29, 1930: Our Lady appeared to her [Berthe] and promised her "nothing but suffering!"

On Good Friday of the following year 1931: "The world is inundated with crime, and there are the sins of priests, and the scandal of immodest fashions. The evils that will break upon the world will be frightful."

February 10, 1932: Three times did the Virgin-Mother place her hand on Berthe's forehead saying: "What suffering! What suffering! What suffering!"

November, 1932: "You are like Me, courageous on your cross, but it is I who give you strength. It is a time of suffering — determined by Me, uncertain for you."

April 27th, 1934: Our Lord told her: "The storm is abating. So many prayers are ascending to me! So many supplications, sincere and ardent, are being sent up to My Heart and through that of My Mother, that I will impose on the mighty one an era of peace, of short duration however, because the spirit of evil does not cease to incite and to goad the pride of any nation which lives only on the thought of revenge and domination."

March, 1938: The Blessed Virgin came to her one night of frightful suffering, and said: "All for my Son! Do not refuse human aid and comfort, your sufferings are beyond human endurance. But I am near you — the Mother who is watching over all your pains which are so pleasing to my Son. Give thanks to God Who has accepted your offering, and taken it for the sanctification of your soul — for that of the clergy, and for the peace of the sad world." Saying this, two big tears fell from the eyes of Our Lady.

1939: "Remain in peace, you are one of my crucified members," Jesus said to her.

End of October, 1939: But the gracious Virgin Mother was there watching: "Your Calvary is not over," she said; "if you did but know how eagerly my Son is gathering your sufferings for the salvation of souls and for the alleviation of the present calamities, not one of them would crush you without being a joy."

September 1st, 1939: "That nation is on the way to its own undoing. It is responsible for its illusory pride."

January 22, 1940: The following words rang in her ears like a death-knell: "Belgium will be invaded."

July 2nd, 1940: "It is hearts that must be changed. This will be accomplished only by the Devotion proclaimed, explained, preached and recommended everywhere. Recourse to My Mother under the title I wish for her universally, *is the last help I shall give before the end of time.*"

November 4, 1941: "The invader is at My Mercy for the punishment he deserves. Justice will be done in everything. The chastisement is rumbling, the leaders feel it coming near, they dread it and they realize that they can do nothing to avert it. It is then that My judgment and the power of My Will shall be made known. My Work will never fall short of achievement. Belgium will again be prosperous."

December 8, 1941: "The safety of your country, internal peace and confidence in My Church will revive through the spread of the Devotion and the Consecration which I wish in order that the Sorrowful and Immaculate Heart of My Mother, united in all to My Heart, may be loved and glorified. Deliverance will thus be the work of our two Hearts, the triumph of our love for the people upon whom this Consecration will bestow confidence according to My promises."

December, 1941: "By confident consecration to My Mother, the Devotion to My Heart will be strengthened and, as it were, completed. This Devotion, this Consecration will be, according to My promise, a renovation for My Church, a renewed strength for Christianity which is too often wavering, a source of signal graces for souls, who thereby will be more deeply penetrated with love and confidence."

"The clear light to be granted, through recourse to My Mother, will bring about, above all, the conversion of a multitude of straying and sinful souls: the pity of the Sorrowful and Immaculate Heart of My Mother will implore Mercy for them from My Heart."

Unknown date: "In order to do good, it is essential that your soul should blossom forth in smiles of kindliness, and this, notwithstanding all your sufferings, because you are the reflection of the qualities of My Heart."

April, 1942: The Savior added: "You will never know any consolation."

April 25th 1942: Our Lord, making allusion to the increasing tempo of the war, said: "A frightful torment is in preparation. It will be seen that the forces launched with such fury, will soon be let loose. It is, now or never, the moment for all of you to give yourselves to the Sorrowful and Immaculate Heart of My Mother. By her acceptance of Calvary My Mother has participated in all My sufferings. Devotion to her Heart united to Mine will bring peace, that true peace, so often implored and yet so little merited."

August 5th: 1942: "You have not the consolation of the gentle visit of My Mother, but you have in its fullness that of My abiding love, and therefore your soul should never know disappointment. Do you not feel this consolation which is the strength of your life? Continue to offer up your life of suffering because it leads to the triumph of My Will. The Heart of My Mother will be understood as it ought to be, and the Devotion to her Heart united to Mine will give peace, but true peace so much sought after and yet so little merited."

1942: Berthe complained thus to Jesus: — "Lord, how is it that, while confiding this work to me, you permit it to be thwarted at every moment?"

"You are astonished!" The Divine Master deigned to answer: "Do you forget that My own acts were constantly thwarted and that My Mother always lived in anxiety and suffering? Remain in your way, in spite of darkness and give time for the light to make its appearance."

Christmas 1942: "When you surrendered yourself to Me as a victim," Jesus said to her, "you not only accepted to be united to my whole life and to My Calvary, but also to My sacred Infancy hidden, poor, miserable, deprived of all, and offered as a holocaust."

1943?: "In the hour of triumph" the Savior had said, "it will be seen that *I alone have inspired,* in my chosen instruments, a Devotion similar to that with which My Heart is honored. IT IS AS A SON THAT I HAVE CONCEIVED THIS DEVOTION IN HONOR OF MY MOTHER. IT IS AS GOD THAT I IMPOSE IT."

APPENDIX

The Reputed Sanctity of Berthe Petit

The reputed sanctity of the apostle of devotion to the Sorrowful and Immaculate Heart of Mary, is well summed up in the following few extracts from the writings of eminent men and women who had been well acquainted with her holy life.

1) Here is the opinion of the Reverend Father Garrigou-Lagrange, O.P., Professor of Theology at the Angelicum (Rome).

ROME, OCTOBER 4, 1951

"I have a vivid remembrance of Berthe Petit whom I saw in Switzerland during the 1914-1918 war. I much appreciated the Devotion to the Sorrowful and Immaculate Heart of Mary. It recalls — as was the viewpoint of Cardinal Mercier and Cardinal Bourne — what the Blessed Virgin has received from God — the grace of Her Immaculate Conception; and also what the Mother of God has done and suffered for us. This invocation seems opportune in these days of universal suffering, as borne out by the consecration made to the Sorrowful and Immaculate Heart of Mary by several Bishops in various dioceses throughout France and Belgium."

2) To quote one of her companions at the boarding school (the convent of the Bernardine Dames of Esquermes who were by now established at Ollignies):

"Her piety was profoundly touching without ostentation. She was very delicate in health, gentle and resigned. She was like a beautiful delicate flower. There was something at once other-worldly and ideal in her character — a contrast to the boisterous joy of her companions."

2) "In 1896, Fr. Masselis, Rector of the Redemptorist Fathers, became her director and remained so until 1908, the year he set out for Rome. He said in 1910:

"In my humble opinion, here is a soul singularly favored by God, and since I have known her, very faithful in following the impulse of grace.

I have found in this chosen soul real and profound humility, absolute purity of heart, invariable obedience and patience that I do not hesitate to call heroic."

"A prey from her youth to bodily infirmity, she has never ceased to suffer, but she has suffered unflinchingly the most acute, often the most atrocious pain. To these sufferings were added heartaches, above all from the day she saw her parents ruined. Thenceforward she devoted herself to them, working unceasingly, despite the extremely painful condition of her health."

"For long years, this generous soul had offered herself by vow for the conversion of sinners and I could never say that her spirit of sacrifice wavered before these extraordinary trials with which God was pleased to visit her."

"She was by nature gifted with a lively and well-trained intelligence, a highly balanced judgment and a generous heart. She used these gifts only in self-forgetfulness and devotedness to others."

"Nothing more discreet than her words, her conduct: nothing more dignified than her bearing: nothing more gentle than her behavior: nothing more edifying than her whole life. She exercised, too, an exceptional influence over those who had to deal with her, and amongst the pious and judicious people who had contact with her (I know a great many) I think that none could be found who did not recognize in the life of Berthe Petit, the seal of real sanctity. Oftentimes Our Lord made her the instrument of His mercy to souls who had strayed away."

"Christian prudence guides this soul who is surely led by grace and I declare that, despite her bodily sufferings and interior trials, this virginal soul, trained in the school of the Holy Spirit, always enjoyed the precious fruit of real and profound peace."

"She is unaware of her merits and this saintly unknowing, which I witnessed so often, and which it was my duty to foster, has revealed the fund of humility with which this soul is endowed. That Our Lord was pleased to shower astonishing favors on her does not at all surprise me."

"By nature calm, well balanced and devoid of all exaltation, she has received these divine favors without being in the least troubled or disconcerted by them; and while no one was more astonished at them than herself, she has but one end in view: to know and accomplish the Holy Will of God as manifested to her."

3) Circumstances brought about the visit to Switzerland of the Reverend Father Frey, Superior of the French Seminary in Rome. It is interesting to hear his impression of Berthe Petit whom he met in Fribourg. We quote his statement here together with that of Father Bohrer, Chaplain of the Institute of St. Agnes at Lucerne.

"I had occasion to see Berthe Petit at Sàrnen, from the 8th to the 12th of August, 1914. I saw her again at Lucerne, from the 7th to the 10th of October of the same year."

"No one ever made an impression on me such as I experienced on meeting her. It seemed to me that I was in the presence of a being more than human. I always found her most recollected and dignified — yet without excess — for she was unfailingly affable. A smile of welcome would light up this countenance, so emaciated, so ravaged by suffering."

"Her conversation was earnest, and she was remarkable for her tact and delicate attentions to those around her: on occasion she would laugh heartily, yet with restraint. Something pure and heavenly emanated from her whole person and commanded respect. I never knew her to fail by the least gesture or word contrary to the most exquisite sweetness, the most delicate charity, the most scrupulous modesty."

"She was ever ready to bestow her kind attentions on her mother who did not even appear to notice them. In everything she acted with utter self-forgetfulness, without the slightest affectation but with utter simplicity."

"She always showed the deepest reverence and the most complete obedience to him whom she called 'Father.' She loved solitude and prayer, and yet she never hesitated in the continual sacrifice of her own taste, in order to give pleasure to her mother or to those with whom she lived."

"For nourishment, I have seen her take a little black coffee with a lump of sugar in the morning. Later, at midday, and occasionally in the evening, she took a little white wine."

"As I was giving her Holy Communion, I noticed that her tongue, heavily coated, was split in the center. She must be suffering from a horrible thirst."

"She has assured me that in one full week she sleeps only about three hours, and at that it is a very light sleep during which she does not completely lose consciousness."

"Her piety is touching: I have seen her, after Holy Communion, with her arms modestly crossed on her breast and head slightly bowed, remaining completely motionless for more than three quarters of an hour. Seeing her thus, one gets an indefinable impression of peace and happiness. It seems as though she were, for a few moments, free from all sufferings, and completely absorbed in God."

"Her sincerity is above all suspicion. In this regard one could not, honestly, have the least mental reservation. It would be doing that soul atrocious injury. Her countenance is open and limpid, without the slightest embarrassment. What she says, she believes with all her soul. When you speak to her about the Devotion to the Sorrowful Heart of Mary, she expresses herself in such a tone of conviction that the listener is entirely convinced. I shall never forget the tone in which she said to me: 'Ah! How much I feel that Our Lord wants to see the Sorrowful Heart of His Mother loved and honored!' You have the conviction of absolute trust in her assertions. Anything like an untruth on her part, would appear an impossibility."

"On the other hand, she is a soul who realizes fully the import of her words. She seems to me to be extremely intelligent. What strikes me specially about her, is the perfect moderation and balance of all her gestures and words. She is never carried away, or unduly hurried. Her judgment is remarkably sure: perfect equilibrium reigns in all her faculties. She is completely self-possessed in all her actions and words. When you remember that she suffers perpetually a real martyrdom from constant headaches, stomach ulcer, burning thirst, etc., you have to admire her serene composure."

"There is no trace of exaltation or gushing enthusiasm about her. She is ruled not by imagination, but by intellect."

"She is perfectly conscious of her exceptional role, and she accepts it, solely because she is convinced that such is the Will of God. She declares that she accepted it only with the greatest repugnance, having begged God to leave her in her obscurity. She has few consolations in her surroundings, and her extraordinary mission brings her only sufferings."

"She says that, of all the crosses Our Lord has placed upon her, this is the heaviest. No matter how deeply you search, you cannot discover any personal motive for the task she is assuming. She asks no better than to be broken, crushed, annihilated - provided that the Sorrowful Heart of Mary be glorified as Jesus wishes."

"To sum up: Confronted with this insoluble problem, you have to admit that you are dealing with a saint and that her statements are to be taken as entirely trustworthy. Furthermore, the moment you come in contact with her, any prejudices you may have had against her, vanish."

4) In 1895 she lost her director, Father Jarlan, who was called to Paris on December 17, 1910. Here is what this religious thought of her. We set out his judgment textually, for it shows to great advantage the work of grace in her soul.

"I declare that I was the spiritual director of Berthe Petit from the year 1888 to 1895. When I first saw her she was eighteen years of age. She had just left the boarding school and was devoting herself to her parents who were then enduring a very severe trial — the loss of their fortune. From that time her life was one of suffering and heroic devotedness. She made every effort to procure some comfort for her beloved parents and to make their lot more bearable. She forgot herself to the detriment of her own health. Several times I saw her at the point of death, but the moment she recovered she would take up her life of sacrifice once more, although she knew that she was thereby exposing herself to relapses."

"Her patience during these illnesses has been admirable; she had special devotion to the Divine Will which she wishes to accomplish perfectly. She is a chosen soul, very high in the ways of God. She thirsts for suffering and her one ambition is to be a living victim, holy and agreeable to God according to the mind of St. Paul."

"Her intelligence is lively, her judgment sure, her prudence remarkable."

"She is very anxious for the sanctification of others. Often I used to put her zeal to the test by confiding to her some souls in whose conversion I was interested. I always had reason to rejoice or rather to thank the Author of every gift for having given such grace to a soul whom I regard as privileged."

"None of the souls whom I confided to her resisted her gentle influence. Two, especially, having led a stormy life in the world, entered religion and there died the death of the predestined. I have often been told that souls are irresistibly penetrated with respect in her presence. However, she does nothing to attract this deference. Her bearing is elegant but withal very simple, her manners are affable and her conversation perfectly natural."

5) It may be opportune here to quote the statement of Father Bohrer, Chaplain to the Institute of St. Agnes at Lucerne, who wrote thus on the 3rd of December, 1914:

"Since the year 1911, I have seen Berthe Petit on several occasions. She was staying in Lucerne with her mother. I have often been received by these ladies, but for the past two months I have had occasion to be in closer contact with Berthe. She was obliged to remain temporarily in Lucerne, for the war had prevented her return to Belgium."

"It is quite obvious that her life is a series of perpetual sufferings, physical and moral, which give her no respite. They are capable of completely crushing one who takes no solid nourishment, but only a little black coffee in the morning and a very small glass of wine at midday. Even this her stomach rejects almost immediately. Yet, this invalid is regularly up and about all day, doing the housework, surrounding her mother with constant care, going out on needful but very fatiguing errands, receiving people who come to her for light and consolation; praying and writing. She is always calm, always affable, always recollected, always even-tempered."

"As for her nights, I can well believe one so truthful and straightforward as Berthe as well as those in her immediate circle when they assure me that the night always means a long and painful insomnia, broken only by a quarter of an hour's sleep. It is easy to see this, for the next morning, Berthe would present herself at the Communion bench, more worn out and crushed physically, than at any other time of the day. However, after Holy Communion, she appears invigorated and ready to begin another full day such as I have described."

"I have sometimes enumerated the various Christian virtues — with this soul in mind — and I cannot but testify that she possessed them all in an eminent degree."

6) From Mlle Marie Madeleine Keusch, one of Berthe's friends, who afterwards became a Sister of Charity of St. Vincent de Paul, at Angers, Soeur Marthe.

"It is with deep emotion that I look back on my acquaintance with this saintly soul. The marvels of her life were all hidden in an exquisite simplicity with which she performed her actions. The labors of her life were directed mainly to the devotion to the Sorrowful and Immaculate Heart of Mary. She spoke of it wherever she went, and to whomsoever she met. I thank Our Lord for having placed Mlle Petit on my way to Him. It was through her that, my vocation was settled and that I became a Sister of Charity."

7) From Mlle Borcart, in religion, Soeur Marie Florentine, Trinitarian, at Vevey.

"At first sight, Mlle Petit would not strike people as a mystic. Of a distinguished and dignified appearance, she was kind and easily approachable, using every opportunity to please others. Her penetrating eyes seemed to reach the bottom of our souls. I am convinced that she remains continually in the presence of God. At times, especially after holy Communion, she was utterly unaware of what was going on around her. She was lost in contemplation with the Lord for an hour or two, and spoke to none. In the midst of a great and habitual suffering, she showed a wonderful spirit, but on certain days — Fridays and the whole of Lent, she suffered much more and was obliged to stay in bed. Her countenance betrayed intense suffering, but her soul remained full of fortitude. If some one were to tell her, "You suffer a great deal," she would quickly answer: "It is very good for me." Her motto was: "Duty first."

Mlle Petit once wrote enclosing a picture of Our Lady: "It was given to me and to my school companion at the Convent of Ollignies when I was 15 years old. I thank God that its influence has remained in my life." She said one day: "From the age of fourteen I have refused nothing to God." These facts sum up all the details I could furnish about the virtues she so faithfully practiced. To follow daily, every inspiration of God's grace! What a tremendous ideal! I therefore, consider that Mlle Petit is a saint. Now that God has called her to Himself, I feel more inclined to pray to her, than for her."

8) From Sister Valesine, Trinitarian, at Vevey, who was in charge of Berthe when she was boarding there during the Great War.

"I can still remember what I noticed in Mlle Petit: in the first place, her miraculous life. When "Our Mother" (Superior) announced her visit, I was somewhat skeptic and said to myself: We shall see. If she does not take her meals in the refectory, sure, she eats elsewhere, in her room perhaps! One cannot live on air! Being rather inquisitive, I made up my mind to watch her. This was easy for me as I was put in charge of her room. I closely observed her for a year, and can assert that she not only lived without food during that period, but also practiced heroic virtues. This soul was a revelation to me! Jesus Christ was personified in her. At times, I would try to place my difficulties before her. With Christ-like sympathy and kindness, she made it easy for me to speak; before I could explain myself, she would tell me in a few words, as to what was troubling me. Often, it was quite unnecessary to speak; she would guess everything. Like myself, all our sisters too had the same experience. She was very humble, always shunning notice, most obedient and child-like. The fact that people came to know of her life without food, was real mortification to her."

9) The following is an extract from the evidence of an Alsacian friend, Madame Baudry, given in 1945.

"...From the beginning of our friendship, I realized what a grace God had bestowed upon me, by sending Berthe as a guardian angel to lead me to Him. What struck me most was her exquisite simplicity and especially, her deep understanding of the difficulties and sufferings of others who, like her, were not called to such heights of holiness.

Berthe came to stay with me in 1927. I can attest that nothing whatsoever was given to her except a little black coffee in the morning, which she rejected shortly afterwards. I can never forget the changing expressions of her beautiful face during her thanksgiving. One could see how she was totally lost in God, far from our miserable world."

10) Berthe was almost eighteen years old when she left Ollignies. "You are taking away everybody's heart," said Dame Marie Hortense, "and you are leaving yours to none." Indeed her heart belonged to God alone. The same Religious spoke thus of her pupil twenty-three years later:

"Berthe Petit was a boarder at Ollignies during the years 1886 and 1887. She was a pious, virtuous girl, delicate of manner and bearing. In those days her health was already very precarious and this prevented her from studying as assiduously as she would have liked."

"I have remained in touch with her since she left school. I always found her very supernatural, accepting trials of health or any others with a perfect submission to the Will of God. She was even happy to suffer for love of Our Lord. She is very reserved on the question of her interior life and she has no pretensions to high spirituality."

"When her parents suffered a great reverse of fortune, she devoted herself to them in every way. Her filial love stopped at nothing; she became not only their breadwinner, but their moral support. After days of hard work she would muster sufficient strength to spend part of the night writing in order to help her father in his office work."

"The marvelous thing is that Berthe has been able, for twenty years, to maintain this laborious task in spite of severe suffering and in the absence of nourishment. She has often been at the last extremity. She surmounted each of her maladies: but they made her increasingly weaker, and ever less capable of working, but always courageous and disposed to accomplish whatever Providence might ask of her."

"I may also mention, especially, her influence over those around her. To see her is to become attached to her and to seek her advice. Her kindness, her obliging charity, full of modesty, touches one deeply; her one wish is to help, to relieve, and to do good to souls."

11) In September, Berthe went to Lourdes with the National Pilgrimage. There she met the Reverend Father Bulliot, Marist, ex-professor of the Catholic Institute of Paris. We see, from his own attestation, the impression the humble pilgrim made upon him. He says:

"My first meeting with Berthe Petit was in one of the chapels adjoining the Rosary Basilica at Lourdes. She and her mother assisted at the Mass I celebrated there. During the whole of that Mass I felt the deepest impression of confusion for my sins that ever I experienced. I saw them in a different light and I promised Our Lord to confess them again in a new general confession. Imagine my surprise when, after Mass, Berthe Petit said: 'During Mass I heard a word which concerns you: "Pray for him, he will soon feel the effect of your prayer." ' She gave me some words of encouragement which, I felt, were appropriate and which appeared to me to come straight from the compassionate Heart of Our Lord."

"I remained under that impression for several weeks and I noticed the calm, the humility and the sweetness with which this child of God spoke to me. It was obvious that she was fully aware of the striking connection between my impressions and her words."

"I mention this only by way of expressing an opinion formed on my own experience."

"How happy I should be if her desire were realized — that of the Consecration of the World to the Sorrowful and Immaculate Heart of Mary!"

12) She was also visited by Countess Gh. de C., lady-in-waiting, who, recalling these hours, wrote as follows on December 12, 1943: —

"I became acquainted with Berthe Petit in 1927, after the death of Monsignor Pieraerts (chaplain to the Royal Court). Being very friendly with him, I often begged his prayers and he said to me on one occasion: "I shall confide your request to a very holy soul to whom Cardinal Mercier sometimes has recourse to obtain graces." But Monsignor Pieraerts never told me her name. Soon after his death, a mutual friend brought Berthe to visit me. The thought struck me: It is Monsignor Pieraerts who sent her to me!"

"Her beautiful eyes, so clear, so full of faith, seemed to see what we could not. What was remarkable in her, was that her physical trials, her terrible sufferings never altered the clearness of her thought or the balance of her judgment. Descending from the heights of contemplation to bend down with sympathy over human miseries she was able to give practical advice to her friends — even in temporal matters."

13) The Reverend Father Kn . . . of the Society of the African Missions, was good enough to give, on June 2, 1943, this attestation which outlines, in a striking way, the Eucharistic life of the servant of God: —

"For six years I brought Holy Communion to Mlle. Petit and I witnessed day to day, to my great edification, what a holy soul she was and how the Eucharist was for her the viaticum of each day. To bring her Holy Communion was my joy. Most probably you think it must be so for any priest, whose principal function is the administration of the Sacraments. But remember, however, that I have been a missionary for many years on the Gold Coast, which is the most trying country on the face of the earth. Its climate can be ruinous to health, and it has not spared mine, so much so that I suffer every day, especially in the morning, from malaria and asthma. It will thus be easily understood how difficult it was to fulfill this priestly ministry towards Mlle. Petit!"

"It was not so much the idea of fulfilling my priestly ministry that gave me this joy, as the fact that I was to bring my Jesus to a soul supernaturalized — one who was living only through Him and suffering for Him alone."

"Having sometimes to replace a member of the parish clergy for one of the regular Masses, it would happen that the patient did not get Holy Communion at the usual hour. I myself felt pain on this account: — I knew that, for many hours, she had been waiting for the Bread of Life with a real "eucharistic hunger." As I drew near the room where she awaited the Host, I could hear her sighing for Holy Communion. As soon as she had received the Sacred Species, the hunger of her soul would be appeased. After each Communion her spirit seemed to leave this world. It was, in fact, the 'great event' of the day. For this she had prepared during the long hours of insomnia and to the very end she lived on the Bread of Life. I shall never forget her last Communion."

"On March 25th, it seemed to me that Mlle. Petit was slightly better. She had found it less difficult than the day before to receive the divine Particle — about the tenth of a normal Host. She was to die, however, on Friday, March 26th. That morning, I had the impression that this would be her last Communion. When I was there with the Sacred Species, close to her lips, she was not immediately aware of my presence. Suddenly she revived and, as usual, joined her hands to receive Holy Communion. She had great difficulty in parting her lips. . . . After Communion, she cried aloud and in a strong voice "I thirst!" Several times she repeated these words of the dying Christ."

"At that moment I understood something of the anguish with which Jesus must have pronounced this word on the Cross. . . . It was the last time that Mlle. Petit received the Blessed Sacrament."

*   *   *   *   *   *   *   *

These and many other testimonies bear witness to the
extraordinary graces bestowed on the servant of God, and to
the value of her authentic message in favor of the devotion
and consecration to the Sorrowful and Immaculate Heart of
Mary.

INDEX

Secret of the Rosary

Publications

Made in the USA
Monee, IL
09 January 2021